ISBN-13: 978-1532753954
ISBN-10: 1532753950

Tatted Earrings & More

By

Rozella Florence Linden

Dedication

For all people who are struggling with a lifestyle
they neither chose nor desire.

Human trafficking is a serious problem in our world
today, and most people do not realize how many
lives are destroyed in order to make money by
the individuals who trade in human flesh.

You can help...

www.humantrafficking.org

This book began as a project for a Christmas party for
women rescued from human trafficking. I was blessed
to participate in it with friends from several non profit
groups working together to give these wonderful ladies a
memorable Christmas holiday party.
I tatted earrings for them.

About the Author

I was born in Warren, Ohio.
Both of my grandmothers tatted, and did other handcrafts.
I learned tatting from my mother. When I was very little she
taught me over and over how to make the tatting DS.
Before I started kindergarten I successfully tatted a ring
that would slide correctly.

I did not do much tatting until I was a teenager when I decided to tat
Christmas presents for my family. My sister also tats, as do some of my
other family members. For years all the people I knew who tatted were
my relatives and people who we had taught to do it.

I wrote my first book, Easy Tatting - Dover Publishing, at the request of
a class of tatting students I taught at Southwest MI College
evening community college.

Rozella Florence Linden is my pen name. I was divorced and did not
wish to publish a book under the last name of my X husband.
Rozella is my maternal grandmother's first name. Florence is my
mother's middle name, and Linden is my sister's favorite tree.

I have been happily married to my sweetheart, Dan Perry for 17 years.

Rozella Florence Linden
AKA Ruth Perry
March 2016

Table of Contents

TOOLS AND SUPPLIES

My Favorite workspace is on our dining room table. My tools and supplies are all handy. If I am doing something simple it can be done in the living room while watching TV.

I have two bead mats, one light colored, and one darker so that I have a good contrast with any project I am making. I have two of my favorite tatting shuttles, scissors, a size 14 crochet hook, a quilter's basting needle to sew in the thread ends, a beading needle for small thread, a quilter's T-Pin, triangular bead tray, a floss threader and a homemade bead stringing wire, a jewelry toolkit, a collapsible trash bin, magnifying glasses, and a magnifying ruler, plus thread and projects in progress.

You should substitute your favorite tatting supplies and make your workspace the way you like it.

Note: I usually do not remove the table centerpiece or other items I have on the table. There is a crocheted chick in the upper right corner as I had been making these to give away at Easter. I often work on multiple projects at one time... Squirrel!!!

Jewelry Findings

There are many different kinds of earring findings available in craft stores and online. I personally like the ones called French hooks. I do not like the kidney wires because they are almost impossible to open, and unacceptable for people with arthritis. The ordinary earring hooks are OK, but they really need a back to be sure you don't loose them. The lever back findings are easy and secure,

Buying in bulk from an online supplier is just smart if you are making lots of earrings to sell. Gift shops that cater to tourists may prefer only jewelry make with real gold or sterling silver findings. Craft fairs or bazaars where you sell from your own booth probably do not care, They just want you to pay them for the space.

Know your market!!! If you only make things for yourself and your friends, then YOU are the market. Make what you want.

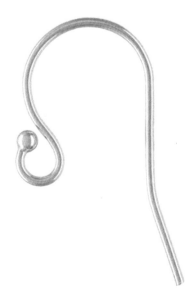

This is a Sterling Silver French Hook ear wire. In silver or 14 ct. gold it is my absolute favorite.

I can put any tatted earring on it by slipping a tatted ring onto the wire, and then change the earrings for a different pair whenever I wish by slipping one off the wire and another onto it.

Awesome! But a bit pricey.

I show my method to attach findings to earrings on page 42. You can just use a jump ring to attach tatted earrings to the findings or you can hang a tatted earring from a small piece of chain with a jump ring.

Jump rings should NEVER be opened by pulling them apart in a manner that makes the circle bigger. Only open them using tools right for the job, and turn one side towards you and the other side away so that when they are closed they are secure and in the same shape as they came.

If you do not know the basics of making jewelry, get a book on the subject. Borrow one from the public library unless you want it for your own collection. Once you read it and learn all the cool stuff you can return it to the library so someone else can read it too.

OK, I'm old, but I love the public library. It was the closest thing we had to Google search in the 50s & 60s, and 70s, and 80s. I love real books! Especially when the power goes off from a storm.

There is probably a You Tube video on just about everything now. There are groups on FB and online as well. But, that's just not where I look first.

I do buy things on Ebay, and sell things on Craigs list. I am a computer geek by education and occupation. In fact, I bought the sterlling silver earring hooks on Ebay for $10 for five pairs of them, plus shipping.

Sometimes I can't find the right tool for the job, and I have to make my own. My friend, Joanne, showed me how to make a bead needle from a piece of beading wire. Take about a six to eight inch long piece of the wire and fold it in half. Use pliers to make the fold compact, then cut the ends so they are even.

I LOVE this tool!!!

THREADS

We are SO lucky these days with all the beautiful colors and kinds of threads available! There are lots of hand dyed thread color combinations, and many different sizes.

I prefer softer thread, like pearl cotton, for anything I am going to wear that will touch my skin. Bracelets, chokers, etc. have to be comfortable to wear, or I won't wear them. I tatted a choker with stiff thread, and it is in a drawer waiting for me to find something else to do with it! After wearing it for a few minutes it was so irritating I took it off.

The stiffer threads are good for paper clip bookmarks, hair clips, earrings, and pendants that don't touch my skin as much. You may agree with me on this or not. I just like comfort - in my old age. <G>

I bought some of the thread that I used for photos in this book recently at the Fingerlakes Tat days. A beautiful variegated blues called Tropical Wave from Karey Soloman is my new favorite thread.

Most of the patterns in this book can be tatted with size 10, 20, 30, 40, and 80 thread depending upon how big you want the finished piece to be. I also use size 8, and 12 Pearle cotton threads in the book, and for tiny intricate designs I use hand quilting thread that has a glaze on it.

Tatting the Celtic knot patterns works better in size 20 or larger thread so that it is easier to see to make the Celtic knot weaving come out right. Magnifiers help.

Color choices are unlimited. If you want to figure out what colors go together without taking a course in design, look to nature. A book of flowers or butterflies will have lots of unusual and beautiful color combinations.

When tatting earrings to sell I make a variety of colors, often local school colors are a good choice, as well as seasonal or holiday colors. Use lots of variety and have fun with color choices!

Match or contrast thread colors with bead colors to make things that grab the eye so people are attracted to your items. Lavender thread with dark purple beads, Stained glass window colors with black thread, Pink, orange, and yellow together look amazing.

Gold or silver findings? Some colors look good with either, and some look better with one, and not the other. Planning color combinations is the most fun!

BEADS & CHARMS

My Daisy Chain Earrings, taught at Fingerlakes Tat Days 2016 introduce a different way to add a bead to the center of a ring. The beaded charms and pendant shown above all use this method to put a bead in the center of the ring.

They are split rings, and the method for adding a bead to the ring is explained in the earring instructions on pp. 36 - 42.

A - Ring with bead in the center and four clusters of three smaller beads.

B - The same with four more beads added between the clusters.

C - Just the single beads, no clusters.

D - Single beads around the ring with a cluster just at the top.

The pendant at the right is a combination of both A & C.

I like the method shown here for finishing most tatting with a final ring. The way I do it there is only one thread end to hide. The charm on the bracelet in the photo on the cover is tatted in this manner. See the Daisy Chain earrings (P 42) to learn this method.

It is important to be sure you use the correct number of stitches to go around a bead when you put the bead in the middle of a ring. Trial and error, or wild guess may not be the best way to figure it out.

Tat a bead gauge for the particular thread and bead that you intend to use. To do this, wind some of the desired thread onto a shuttle, not much, say 15 turns around the shuttle bobbin or post. Do NOT cut the thread from the ball (Continuous Thread Method CTM).

Tie an overhand knot in the thread between the shuttle and ball. Then, make the first DS a picot's distance from the knot, shown below. Make a Picot every other stitch so the number of stitches is easy to count by twos. The bottom (teal) photo shows the first few DS tatted but the thread not pulled snug yet. The middle (purple) photo shows a few more stitches and the core thread pulled snug. The knot keeps the picot space open.

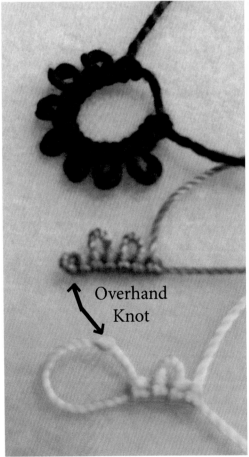

Overhand
Knot

The top photo (black)shows the core thread inserted through the beginning picot.

Place your bead in the center and count the picots to determine how many stitches will fit exactly around your bead with that thread. Sizes differ by brand. Size 20 in Anchor brand thread is not the same as size 20 Lizbeth.

You can pull the thread out of the picot to tat more DS if needed. When you have determined the right number of stitches to use, write it down. Half of the stitches go on one side of the split ring, and half on the other. Add picots or beads in the ring as desired. Needle tatters, use a paper clip at the beginning instead of a knot.

FINISHING AND PRESENTATION

In my opinion tatting that is properly designed, tatted with good consistent tension, and made with good quality thread should not really need much blocking to get the proper shape.

That said, there is good reason to stiffen jewelry items so they keep their shape in normal use. Mine often get stuffed in a baggie in my purse, thrown into my jewelry box, and at times left on the night stand and knocked onto the floor.

People used to stiffen doilies with sugar water. Just imagine the fun someone would have with the bugs here in FL wearing something soaked in sugar... NOT happening!

There is a product called Mary Ellens Best Press. It comes in scented and unscented. Spray it on and finger press it in shape, then let it dry. It is a starch alternative product, but doesn't make the piece very stiff.

http://maryellenproducts.com/Best-Press-Caribbean-Beach-The-Clear-Starch-Alternative.html

Another product is called Aleenes fabric stiffener & draping liquid. It is available on Amazon.com.

Spray starch can be used, but tends to flake off if applied too thick.

You can use a mixture of half Epsom Salt and water to stiffen items without attracting bugs.

Tatting made with the hand quilting thread can be dipped in hot water, then pressed between clean cloths with a hot iron, then let cool. The glaze melts and then bonds together to hold everything in place nicely.

I do not like glue for stiffening tatting. In the Florida humidity it would probably stay sticky all the time.

Hiding Ends

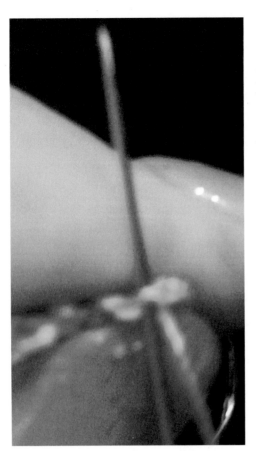

I use a quilter's basting needle, or a beading needle (for small thread) to sew back and forth through the tatting stitches as shown here.

Once you have sewn through three to five stitches (back & forth 6 to ten times) hold the tatting between your thumb and finger and gently but firmly pull on the thread end.

You will feel the thread "POP" into the core of the stitches, and the tatting will <u>NOT</u> look lumpy.

The bottom photo shows the tatting after the thread end is pulled tight. The stitches actually look a bit more compact than the rest of the tatting. You can give it a little tug to loosen up the stitches a bit.

The magic thread trick is fine when sewing two thread ends into the same place in the tatting, but I always sew the end back and forth through the tatting to hide one thread end!

In the bottom photo the thread end is ready to be cut off close to the work.

DESIGNS IN THIS BOOK

The first few designs in this book, pages 10 to 23, are fairly easy to tat and should be great for beginners and advanced beginners.

The patterns on pages 24 to 48 are intermediate to advanced level tatting projects. I introduce a different way to put a bead in the center of a ring.

I also do a similar method to attach a jewelry finding with a split ring, so that there is only one thread end to hide because the other end is hidden in the stitches of the second half of the split ring.

The patterns on pages 49 to 57 are Celtic tatting. These can be fun and a bit more challenging. Enjoy the challenge!

I have never seen a tatting pattern that can not be done by needle tatting.

However, needle tatters must be able to work from shuttle tatting instructions to tat the patterns in this book.

SAND DOLLAR MOTIF & EARRINGS

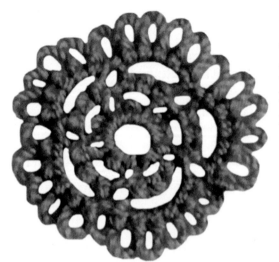

This sand dollar is a beginner level pattern that can be tatted in different sizes. It is just one ring, chains, picots, and joins.

The smaller size is perfect for an earring. Beads may be added to the picots for a bit of bling.

IMPORTANT!!!

Tat with CORRECT Tension

Make sure that this lays flat on each round!!!

One shuttle and ball CTM. Continuous Thread Method means do not cut the thread between the shuttle and ball.

Center Ring (2 – 2 – 2 – 2 – 2) turn

The center ring may either be a true ring or a mock ring for needle tatting.

This sample is needle tatted!

Leave a small space about the size of a joining picot between the ring and the first stitch of the chain.

Round 2 Chain 3 + 3 + 3 + 3 + 3 [these joins are all lock joins made with the shuttle thread]

Join to the small thread space, but do only the first half of a lock join.

Do not tat the second half of the DS. Leave the space of a picot and then tat the next full DS.

To make the smaller motif, tat the next round with a picot between each DS, or a bead between each DS. If you wish to add the beads, put them on the ball thread before beginning to wind the shuttle. Or you may cut the thread from the ball after the previous round, leaving enough thread to tat the last round, and then string the beads on as needed.

Round 3 Chain 5 + 5 + 5 + 5 + 5

Join to the small thread space, but do only the first half of a lock join. Do not tat the second half of the DS. Leave the space of a picot and then tat the next full DS.

Round 4 Chain 4 + 4 + 4 + 4 + 4 + 4 + 4 + 4 + 4 + 4

Join to the small thread space, but do only the first half of a lock join. Do not tat the second half of the DS. Leave the space of a picot and then tat the next full DS.

Round 5 Chain 5 + 5 + 5 + 5 + 5 + 5 + 5 + 5 + 5 + 5 Make picots between each stitch or add beads between each stitch in this round. Cut from the ball and shuttle and tie the ends in the space at the beginning of this round. Hide the ends and then cut close to the work.

TEARDROP EARRING

This is a simple traditional tatted motif. Shown here with and without beads. It is just rings, chains, and joins. The ring at the top may be tatted as a split ring , as shown here, or as a simple ring. With a split ring both ends will be at the top of the motif, with a simple ring both ends will be at the bottom of the last (top) ring.

Wind about 1.5 yard of thread on a shuttle, CTM.

Begin a chain with a picot by tying a knot in the thread between the ball and shuttle and tat the first stitch a picot's distance from the knot.

Start tatting where indicated on photo.

Chain 2 turn
Ring A (3 – 2 – 2 – 3 – 3) turn
Chain 3 turn
Ring B (2 + 3 + 3 – 3 – 3 – 2) turn
Chain 3 turn
Ring C (2 + 3 + 4 – 4 – 3 – 2) turn
Chain 3 turn
Ring D (2 + 3 + 5 – 5 – 3 – 2) turn
Chain 3 turn
Ring E (2 + 3 + 6 – 6 – 3 – 2) turn
Chain 3 turn

Ring F (2 + 3 + 5 – 5 – 3 – 2) turn
Chain 3 turn
Ring G (2 + 3 + 4 – 4 – 3 – 2) turn
Chain 3 turn
Ring H (2 + 3 + 3 – 3 – 3 – 2) turn
Chain 3 turn
Ring I (3 + 3 + 2 – 2 – 3) turn
Chain 2 +
(this join is to the beginning picot)

You may add a drop bead in the center, and beads to the joining and decorative picots if you wish.

A cluster of three beads on each of the decorative picots look very nice. String 27 beads on the shuttle thread. Set 3 beads aside for after the final split ring is closed.

To finish, string two beads on one thread end, and one bead on the other. Put the thread end that has one bead through the second bead of the other thread but from the opposite direction to make the three beads at the top ring. Add an earring finding.

Split Ring J (3 + 4 / 3 + 4)
      Cut the thread ends to about 10 to 15 inches long.

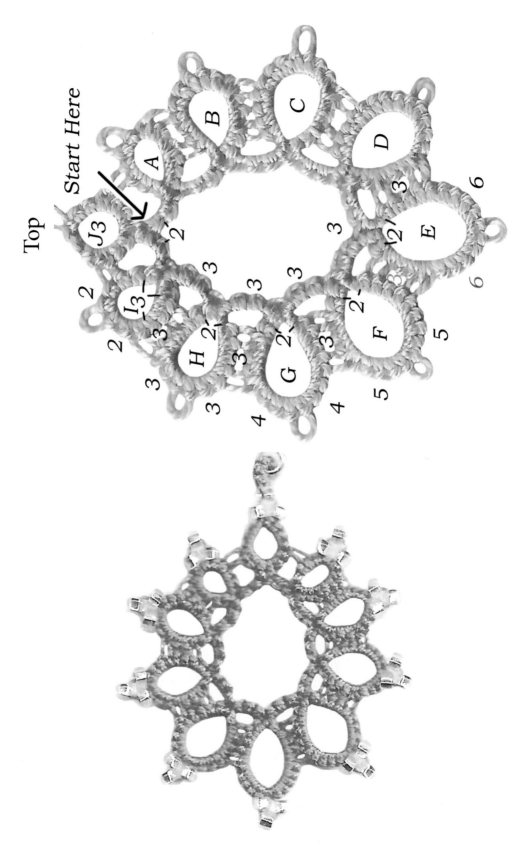

The sample here has 30 seed beads added to the rings.

13

SERENDIPITY SPIRAL EARRING

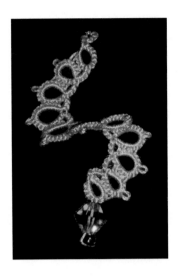

This design kind of just happened. While I was tatting the teardrop earring I noticed the way the partially completed tatting hung from my hand. It gave me the idea that it would make a beautiful 3-D spiral.

Adding a drop bead assembly to the bottom (first) ring gives it a little weight to hold its shape.

Begin with the ring at the bottom which has a crystal drop bead or whatever you wish to put there to give it a bit of weight and sparkle.

I put the crystal bead on the thread, a seed bead, and then went back through the crystal bead before winding the thread on the shuttle. This bead assembly goes in the hand ring of the first ring, so it should be between the ball and shuttle after winding the shuttle, CTM.

First Ring (3 Bead assembly 3 - 3 - 3)

The remaining stitch counts are the same as the Teardrop Earring except that after the ring with 6 DS tat one with 7 DS, then another with 6. Since this one is longer, it will not lie flat.

The final ring at the top can be a normal ring, or a split ring so that there is only one thread end to hide.

The instructions for ending an earring with this method are included with the Daisy Chain Earrings on pp. 38 - 42.

Add beads to the decorative picots and the joining picots if you wish.

14

PAISLEY EARRING

This design reminds me of a paisley print on fabric. The sample here is size 8 Pearle cotton thread, and it measures about an inch tall. Beads may be added to the picots if desired.

One shuttle and ball CTM.

String one seed bead, one pearl, one seed bead onto the ball thread. Go back through the pearl and the first seed bead. Slide the beads a couple of yards onto the ball thread, and then wind about a yard of thread onto the shuttle.

Begin with the ring (5 - 5) turn

Chain 2 - 2 - 2 - 2 - 2 - 2 - 2 - 2 - 2 - 2 - 2 - 2 - 2 [12 picots]
Join to the picot of the ring, but, do just the first half of a shuttle lock join, and then do a SLT
      SLT: Shoe Lace Trick, means
      tie a knot in the two threads.

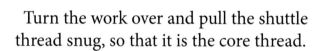

Turn the work over and pull the shuttle thread snug, so that it is the core thread.

Do the second half of the DS.

Slide the beads into place.

Chain 2 + 2 + 3 + 3 + 3 + 3 + 3 + 9 + 3 + 3 + 2 + 2

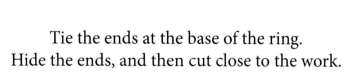

Tie the ends at the base of the ring.
Hide the ends, and then cut close to the work.

Use a jump ring to add an earring finding.

SPIRAL EARRING

One shuttle and ball CTM.
Begin this earring with a Josephine Ring. A ring with one full DS at the beginning and the end of the ring, but just the first half of the DS for the rest of the ring.

The abbreviation for the first half of the stitch is just the letter D. The abbreviation for just the second half of the stitch is the letter S. D first half, S second half. "DS" is the full
tatting stitch or Double Stitch.

Josephine Ring (1 DS, 10 D, 1 DS) turn

Chain 5 - 2 - 2 [continue repeating the - 2 until there are 20 picots, ending with 2 DS.] The tension of this chain has to make the spiral shape. Pull the core thread quite tight so that it looks like the sample.

Ring (5 + 2 - 2)
Ring (2 + 10 - 2)

Tat this next split ring around an earring finding, or use a jump ring to attach it to the finding.
Split Ring (2 + 2 / 5)

You may make another final split ring with 3 / 3 that allows you to only have one end to hide as in the other projects in this book, shown on p. 42.

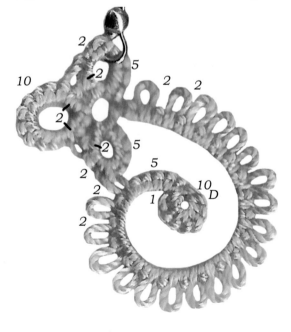

Hide the ends and cut close to the work.

SQUARE MOTIF EARRING

There are many vintage tatting books with patterns that just beg to be made into earrings.

This is a very old motif adapted for an earring.

The beads are optional. and more beads can be added to the decorative picots.

"B+" means Put a bead on the picot when doing the join.

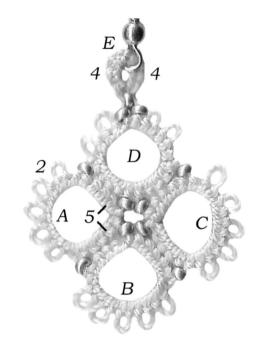

String 3 seed beads onto the shuttle thread. Wind a shuttle with about a yard of thread. Cut from the ball, leaving about 12" of thread tail.

Ring A (5 - 2 - 2 - 2 - 2 - 2 - 2 - 5)
Slide a bead from the shuttle next to the completed ring,

Ring B (5 B+ 2 - 2 - 2 - 2 - 2 - 2 - 5)
Slide a bead from the shuttle next to the completed ring.

Ring C (5 B+ 2 - 2 - 2 - 2 - 2 - 2 - 5)
Slide a bead from the shuttle next to the completed ring.
String a bead onto the tail.

Split Ring D (5 B+ 2 - 2 - 2 / 5 B+ 2 - 2 - 2)

String two beads on one thread end and one bead on the other. Put the thread with one bead through the second bead on other thread, but from the opposite direction.

Split Ring E (4 /4) or just a ring of 8 DS. See page 42 to make the split ring with just one end to hide.

BEADED CHRISTMAS TREE EARRING

This little tree is small but easy to tat. The sample is size 80. You can tell by the earring finding, it is very tiny.

In size 80 thread it is about ¾ inch tall. The beads are size 11 seed beads. String five beads on the shuttle thread, and set five beads aside to use when joining with the beads. You may add more beads and picots for more decorations if you wish.

I have used gold colored seed beads, but it would look good with a variety of color beads or any single color beads, kind of like a real Christmas tree.

B is slide a bead into the tatting. You have to put the bead in the hand ring to do this in a ring. B+ means join with a bead on the picot.

String 5 beads on the thread, and then wind a yard or so onto a shuttle CTM (do not cut from the ball). The beads go on the shuttle thread.

Begin with a picot by tying a knot in the thread between the ball and shuttle. Make the first DS a picot's distance from the knot. This will make a small picot at the beginning of the chain to join to later.

Chain – 1 turn

Ring (2 – 2 – 1 B 2 – 2) turn

Chain 2 – 2 turn

Ring (3 B+ 3 – 1 – 7 – 2)
Ring (2 + 2 BBB 2 – 2)
Ring (2 + 7 – 1 – 3 – 3) turn

Chain 2 B+ 2 turn

Ring (2 B+ 2 B 1 – 2 – 2) turn

Chain 1 + This join is to the beginning picot.
Add the earring finding to the core thread for the split ring.

Split Ring (2 B+ 2 – 4 / 2 B+ 2 – 4)

When the tatting is finished you may sew on more beads,

and a garland of sparkle thread if you wish.

Have fun decorating your tree!

TINY HEART EARRING

This tiny tatted heart is perfect to sew on a special baby outfit, or as ear rings and a pendant for a child.

The sample here is size 20 thread with small pearl beads. The one below is tatted in size 80 thread with size 11 seed beads. I think it would look better with smaller seed beads.

Slide three beads onto the thread of a shuttle wound with any size and color of thread. The beads should be just large enough to string on the thread. The picots between rings are all very small ones. The three picots in the center of the bottom ring are medium, larger, medium.

Ring 1 (2 – 2 – 2)

Ring 2 (2 + 3 – 2)
Join to the last picot of the previous ring.
Repeat Ring 2 three more times.

Slide a bead next to the ring just made.

Slide a bead onto the hand ring thread used to make this next ring.

Ring (3 + 3)

Close the ring with the bead at the bottom of the ring between the first and last stitch.

Slide a bead next to the ring just made. (See photos)

Ring (2 + 3 – 2)

This one is the same as Ring 2 & it joins to the same picot as the last ring.

There are three rings joined together here.

Repeat Ring 2 three more times.

Ring (2 + 2 – 2)

Repeat this ring one more time.

Ring (2 + 3 – 1 – 1 – 3 – 2)

This is the point at the bottom of the heart.

Ring (2 + 2 + 2)

This is the last ring. It is joined to the previous ring and the first ring. It's a bit tricky to do the last join.

Tie the ends together and hide them, and then cut close to the work.

You may wish to use a crochet hook to insert into the picots around the outside of the heart to open them up slightly and pull the rings closer together. See the photo of the very small heart for this effect.

SNOWFLAKE EARRING

Sometimes the most beautiful designs are the simplest ones. This snowflake shows the beauty of tatted lace in a very simple design.

You will need two shuttles, each wound with a yard or so of thread, CTM.

Continuous Thread Method. Wind one shuttle and then pull enough thread from the ball to wind the other shuttle. Cut the thread from the ball, and wind the second shuttle so that the thread is continuous from one shuttle to the other.

Shuttle 1 Split Ring (3 / The rest is the second half of the split ring.
Shuttle 2 Thrown off ring (5 - 5 - 2 - 2 - 5)
On split ring core thread 3
Thrown off ring (5 + 5 - 2 - 2 - 5)
On split ring core thread 3
Thrown off ring (5 + 5 - 2 - 2 - 5)
On split ring core thread 3
Thrown off ring (5 + 5 - 2 - 2 - 5)
On split ring core thread 3
Thrown off ring (5 + 5 - 2 - 2 - 5)
On split ring core thread 3)
Close the Split Ring.

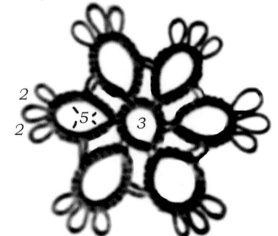

Sixth thrown off split ring (5 + 5 - 2 - 2 - 5 / 5)
Close this split ring and tie the ends through the first picot of the first thrown off ring.

Hid the ends, then cut close to the work.

This snowflake earring will go onto a French Hook earring finding by any center decorative picot.

BEAD CENTERED SNOWFLAKE EARRING

This snowflake has a bead at the center of the motif.

Seed beads can be added to the joining picots and the decorative picots.

String one bead onto the thread, and then wind about a yard of thread onto a shuttle. The bead goes on the shuttle thread.

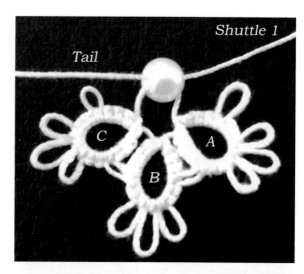

Leave about 24" tail and cut the thread from the ball.

Ring A (4 - 3 - 1 - 1 - 3 - 4)
Ring B (4 + 3 - 1 - 1 - 3 - 4)
Ring C (4 + 3 - 1 - 1 - 3 - 4)

Slide the bead next to the tatting, and put the tail through the bead from the opposite direction. Tie the tail thread to the thread on a shuttle (Shuttle 2).

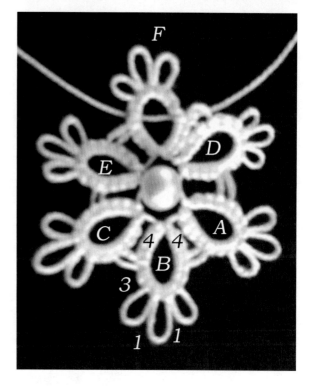

Shuttle 1
Ring D (4 + 3 - 1 - 1 - 3 - 4) The join is to Ring A picot.
Shuttle 2
Ring E (4 + 3 - 1 - 1 - 3 - 4) The join is to Ring C picot.

Split Ring F (4 + 3 - 1 - 1 - 3 / 4) Close the ring and tie the ends through the picot of Ring D. Hide the ends then cut them close.

BEADED SNOWFLAKE EARRING

This pretty snowflake is about an inch across, tatted in size 20 thread with clear seed beads and an ice blue translucent E bead at the center.

There are clusters of four seed beads at the points, and seed beads on the joining picots between the rings.

String 20 seed beads onto the thread, and then the E bead and 3 more seed beads. Wind shuttle 1 and put the 3 seed beads, the E bead, and then 5 more seed beads on Shuttle 1.

Pull a couple of yards of the thread from the ball, and then cut it. Wind Shuttle CTM. The thread is continuous between the two shuttles. The rest of the seed beads go on Shuttle 2.

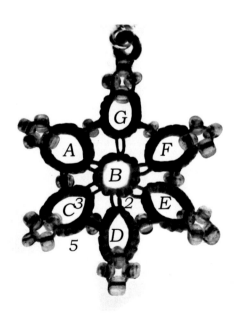

[Shuttle 1] Put 3 beads in the hand ring

Ring A (3 – 5 – BBB, slide a bead from the shuttle, 5 – 3)

Split Ring B (2 /

[Shuttle 2]   2 DS on Core turn

Thrown off Ring C (3 + 5 BBB, slide a bead from the shuttle, 5 – 3)

Turn 2 turn   Thrown off Ring D (3 + 5 BBB, slide a bead from the shuttle, 5 – 3)

Turn   Lay the S1 thread along the Ring B core thread and tat over both threads 2 turn

Thrown off Ring E (3 + 5 BBB, slide a bead from the shuttle, 5 – 3)

Turn 2 turn   Thrown off Ring F (3 + 5 BBB, slide a bead from the shuttle, 5 – 3)

Turn 2 turn   Close the ring with the E bead in the center as in the Daisy Chain earrings on pp. 38 - 42.

Split Ring G, One seed bead in the hand ring. (3 + 5 / 3 + 5)

When this ring is closed there will be one bead at the top. Put 2 seed beads on one thread end, and one on the other. Put the thread end with one bead through the second bead on the other thread end but from the opposite direction. This forms the four-bead cluster at the top.

Finish with a Ring or Split Ring and an earring finding. Hide ends, and then cut close to the work.

FLOWER EARRINGS

This flower tatted in red makes a perfect Christmas Poinsettia. It may be tatted in other colors or variegated to be a Spring, Fall or Summer Flower.

There are beads around the center, but beads may also be added to the joining and decorative picots as in the beaded flower on the next page.

Two shuttles CTM. String six seed beads onto the thread, then wind shuttle 1. Shuttle 1 gets 2 of the beads. Pull enough thread from the ball to wind shuttle 2 (a yard or so). The other four beads go on shuttle 2.

Begin with Shuttle 1
Ring (3 - 5 - 1 - 1 - 5 - 3)
Split Ring (1 B 1 /

Shuttle 2
The rest of this split ring is the second half with thrown off rings.

1 B 1
Thrown off Ring (3 + 5 - 1 - 1 - 5 - 3) turn
1 B

lay the shuttle 1 thread around next to the core thread and tat over the two core threads. This progress is shown in the photo above.
1 turn
Thrown off Ring (3 + 5 - 1 - 1 - 5 - 3) turn
1 B 1 turn
Thrown off Ring (3 + 5 - 1 - 1 - 5 - 3) turn
1 B 1 turn

Pull on the shuttle 1 thread to identify the outside core thread loop, which will get smaller as shown here.

Pull on the smaller loop to close the larger, inside, loop.

Slide the remaining bead from shuttle 1 into the center of the ring, and put both shuttles through the remaining loop of core thread. Pull shuttle 1 thread to close the remaining loop and the ring.

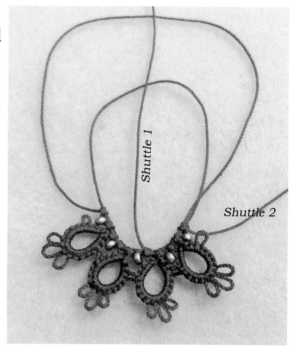

You will have a center ring with a bead in the middle and 5 beads around with 4 thrown off rings. See the photo above.

Split Ring (3 + 5 - 1 - 1 - 5 / 3) Tie the ends through the Ring 1 picot, and then hide the ends and cut close to the work.

BEADED FLOWER

This variation of the flower earring shown in the photo at the right, also has beads on the joining picots and a cluster of three beads at each petal point.

Put 5 Beads on Shuttle 1. Shuttle 2 gets 13 Beads. There are 5 beads on the joining picots, and 3 Beads at the top of the final split ring.

Rings have (3 ∓ 6 BBB 6 - 3)

The ∓ means tat a picot the first time and then do joins in the repeats.

The photo on the right shows this beaded flower with the first four petals completed, and ready to close the center ring.

I have pulled the shuttle one thread to make one core loop smaller.

Next, pull the smaller loop to close the larger loop.

Slide the last bead from shuttle 1 into the center of the ring.

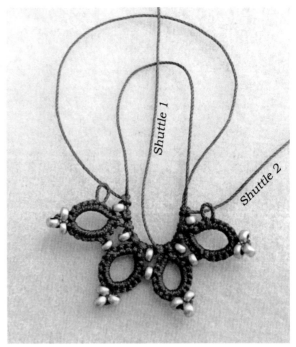

Drop both shuttles through the loop, and then pull shuttle 1 thread to completely close the ring.

Tat the fifth Split Ring.

Split Ring (3 + 6 / 3 + 6)
Cut the thread ends to about 12", and then string 2 beads onto one thread and 1 bead on the other. Put the thread end with one bead through the second bead on the other thread, but from the opposite direction as shown here.

Tighten the threads so the beads make a cluster.

Put an earring finding on one thread and tat around the finding.
Split Ring (4 / put the end through the finding and lay it along the core thread. Tat 4 stitches over both threads. Pull S1 thread to make one loop smaller, and then pull the smaller loop to close the larger loop. Put the S2 thread through the loop & close it. Hide S2 end. Cut.

VARIGATED BEADED FLOWER EARRING

Flowers can be made in other colors and variegated for Spring, Summer, or Autumn flowers.

Here is another flower earring tatted in size 20 variegated thread that just screams -
> "Salsa dancer!"

There are clusters of four beads at the point of each petal, and a size E bead at the center. With beads on the joining picots, and even beads on the small ring tatted around the earring finding, it has lots of bling!

One shuttle with 22 seed beads on the thread wound with a yard or so of any thread you choose. Leave a tail about 12" long

Begin by putting a loop of the thread through the hole in a size E bead. Next, put the bead through the loop forming a larks head knot (DS) on the E bead.

Put 4 of the seed beads in the hand ring and tat the first ring.
Ring (2 - 10 BBB Slide one bead from the shuttle next to the tatting. 10 - 2) When you close the ring there will be one seed bead at the bottom of the ring and four at the point (three up beads and one down bead at the point of the petal).

Tat one Dora Young knot, AKA larks head knot on the E bead. After her patent expired people started calling this a split chain stitch or bridging stitch.

To make the stitch on the E bead pull a loop of the thread up through the bead, put the shuttle through this loop and then pull the loop back down through the bead pulling the shuttle thread to the back.

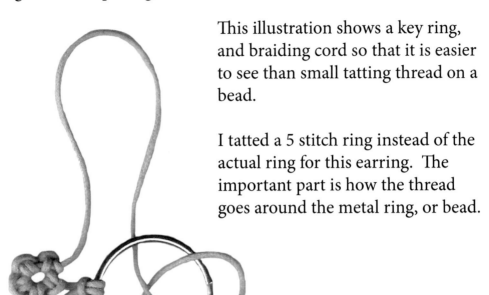

This illustration shows a key ring, and braiding cord so that it is easier to see than small tatting thread on a bead.

I tatted a 5 stitch ring instead of the actual ring for this earring. The important part is how the thread goes around the metal ring, or bead.

Shuttle thread loop - pull to the back.

Take hold of the shuttle thread loop from the back, and gently tighten the half hitch that is made around the bead which is the first half of the DS. Put the shuttle through the loop, and then tighten the second half of the DS.

In this photo the first half of the stitch is formed, and the shuttle put through the loop to make the second half of the stitch. Now just tighten it up.

You may want to practice these on a plastic ring with thick thread a bit so that you can do it easily before working with tatting thread on a bead.

Put 4 of the seed beads in the hand ring and tat the first ring.
Ring (2 B+ 10 BBB Slide one bead from the shuttle next to the tatting.
10 - 2)

The +B means put a bead on the picot for the join between the rings.

Do another stitch onto the center bead, another ring, and repeat 2X so that you have four rings, and five stitches on the center bead.

The fifth ring is a split ring. Put 2 beads in the hand ring.

Split Ring (2 B+ 10 / slide one bead to the bottom of the ring, then tat the second half of the split ring. 2 +B 10)

When this ring is closed there will be one bead at the bottom of the ring, and one at the top.

Cut the ends to about 15" long, and put 2 beads on one thread end, and one on the other as in the previous beaded earring pattern. Put the thread with one bead through the second bead on the other thread but from the opposite direction.

Finally, Make the Split Ring with the earring finding and beads. Put the earring finding on one of the thread ends, and three beads in the hand ring.

Split Ring (1 B 1 B 1 B / Put the S1 thread through the finding as in the previous pattern. Lay S1 thread along the core thread and tat the second half of the Split Ring over both threads. 1 B 1 B 1)

Pull S1 thread to make one core loop smaller. Pull the smaller loop to close the larger loop. Put the S2 end through the remaining loop.

Pull S1 thread to close the ring.

Hide the S2 end, and cut both ends close to the work. By tatting over the S1 thread, there is only one end to hide. The S1 thread end is already hidden in the second half of the ring. See P. 42.

DONUT BEAD PENDANT

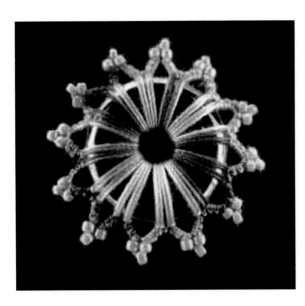

This is size 80 variegated thread on a small hematite donut bead.

I tatted this one as a gift for Bobbie Demmer. She had such an influence on our craft, and is greatly missed!

It has 12 points, but any number of points on any type of donut bead looks nice.

One shuttle and ball CTM. String the number of seed beads needed onto the ball thread, and then wind the shuttle, CTM.

Follow the instructions in the previous pattern to tat the stitches on the donut bead.

Begin a chain with a picot by tying a knot between the ball and shuttle. Tat the first DS a picots distance from the knot.

Chain - 3 , 1 stitch on bead, 1 DS, one stitch on bead.
3 BBB 3, 1 stitch on bead, 1 DS, one stitch on bead.
Repeat desired number of times.

Push the stitches on the bead close together as you tat, and then when you are finished, spread them around the donut bead evenly.

After tatting the last chain 3 section, tie the ends in the first picot, and add two beads on one thread end, and one bead on the other. Put the thread end with one bead through the second bead on the other thread end, but from the opposite direction to make the final three bead cluster at the top.

The hematite beads make a nice pendant, but are a bit heavy for earrings, however, there are donut beads that are not too heavy to make earrings.

Add jewelry findings as in the other patterns in this book.

Hide the ends, and then cut close to the work.

Six, five, and four point samples.

These are the same idea, but slightly different in the stitch count and beads used. The donut beads are semi precious stone, or shell, or any material that you wish to use.

There is not really enough difference to make it a "new" pattern.

Chain -3,
One stitch on donut bead,

1 DS, B, 1 DS
One stitch on donut bead.

Chain 3, BBB, 3 DS
One stitch on donut bead

Repeat desired number of times, and then finish with chain 3.

Tie the ends in the beginning picot and add the three bead cluster at the point as in the other patterns in this book. Hide the ends and cut close to the work. Add jewelry findings for a pendant or earrings.

BUTTERFLY EARRING

This pretty little butterfly has tatted wings and a beaded body. Wind a yard or so of thread onto a shuttle. This variegated is size 20.

This earring is on a French hook which is more secure on a picot than other findings.

BDS is a Balanced Double Stitch.

Wings

Ring (8 BDS 1 DS - 2 - 2 - 8 - 3)
Ring (3 + 8 - 8 - 3)
Leave a space about the size of the last picot.
Ring (3 + 8 - 8 - 3)
Ring (3 + 8 - 2 - 2 - 1 DS 8 BDS)

Body
String one seed bead onto about 20" of a piece of thread at about the middle. This can be whatever color you wish to use to tat the antennae. String one more seed bead onto both thread ends.

Put one thread end under the picot between the bottom wings, and one on top. String both thread ends through one more seed bead. Put one thread end under the thread space between the lower wings, and one on top. Put one seed bead on both thread ends.

Put the thread ends from the body and from the wings through a larger bead. These are pearls. Pull all the thread ends so that they are even, and the butterfly wings and body look right.

Tie all of the thread ends in a double overhand knot. Using two thread ends for each antennae, Chain 1 - 10 and then tie these ends in an overhand knot. Tat the other antennae, joining to the picot.

34

PAPERCLIP BUTTERFLY

This butterfly on a paperclip is tatted with size 10 thread. It is the same as the earring butterfly, except, instead of 8 stitches in the pattern it has 10.

It is joined to the paperclip instead of the picot and the join to the picot in the lower wings,

The space between the two lower wings is about the width of the paperclip. See the photo at the bottom.

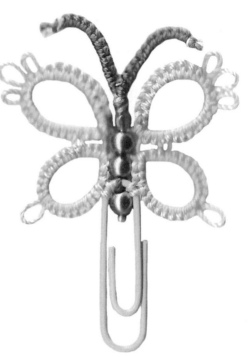

When using larger thread, it will require beads with a larger hole.

String one body bead and then a seed bead on a piece of thread that is about a yard long. Slide the seed bead to the center of the thread.

Take the other thread end through the body bead, under the paperclip, and then through another body bead.

Put the second thread end through the body bead, under the thread space between the lower wings and then through the third body bead.

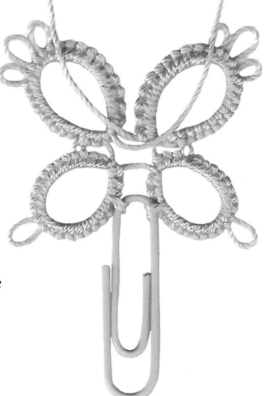

Put all four threads through the fourth body bead, and continue as in the butterfly earring.

DAISY CHAIN EARRING

This pattern requires two shuttles and uses a different method for adding a bead to the center of a split ring.

The sample shown here is tatted with Venus thread size 20, size 15 seed beads, and larger, size E, beads for the center of the flowers.

String nine seed beads on the thread, and then one E bead, three seed beads, one E bead, three seed beads, one E bead, and three more seed beads.

Wind about a yard of thread onto a shuttle, and then pull a couple yards of thread from the ball. Cut the thread from the ball and wind a yard onto another shuttle CTM.

The first nine seed beads go on shuttle 2, and the rest of the beads go on shuttle 1. Begin tatting with shuttle 1 (with the larger beads.)

Shuttle 1 Split Ring (2 – 2 – 2 – 2 – 2 /

After tatting the first half, lay the shuttle thread along the core thread around the hand, and tat the second half of the split ring over both threads: – 2 – 2 – 2 – 2 - 2)

The photo below shows this split ring with the first three DS of the second half completed. Notice, there are two threads in the core of the second half of the split ring.

For illustration purposes this ring is shown smaller than what will go around the hand. The actual split ring has a normal size hand ring.

The thread in this sample is large braiding cord.

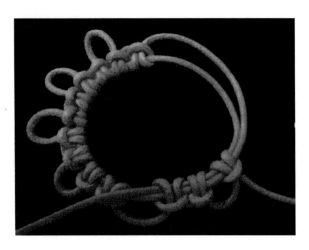

To close the ring, pull the shuttle 1 thread so that one loop of the thread around the hand becomes smaller (left photo). Then, pull on the thread of the smaller loop so that the larger loop closes.

Slide the first E bead into the middle of the ring and hold it in place. (right) Put both shuttles through the remaining loop. (bottom)

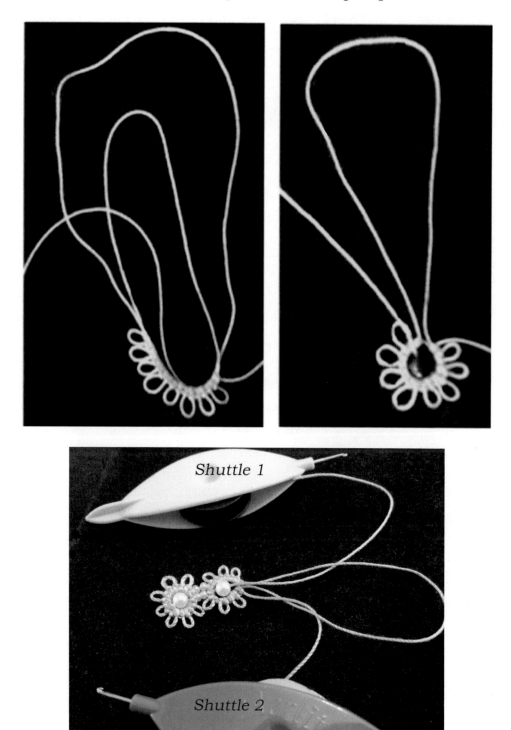

Shuttle 1

Shuttle 2

Finally, pull the Shuttle 1 thread so that the ring closes around the bead in the middle. Gently tighten both shuttle threads so that any slack in the thread is gone.

Slide three seed beads from each shuttle down next to the first flower.

Tat the second flower.

Split Ring (2 – 2 – 2 – 2 – 2 /

Lay the shuttle thread along the core thread as before, and tat the second half of the split ring over both threads.
2 – 2 – 2 – 2 – 2)

Follow the same procedure to put the bead in the center and close the ring as in the first flower.

Repeat the second flower one more time to tat the third flower. Slide the last of the seed beads down and tat a small ring to add the earring finding.

Tat a second earring.

This same pattern can be followed to tat a matching bracelet and necklace with endless variations by adding a second round to the work.

Adjust the stitch counts to fit the beads used, and personal preference.

BEADED DAISY CHAIN SET

The earring, bracelet, and charm above have beads instead of picots. To tat a matching pendant, make another earring, but with a jump ring instead of an earring finding.

These have just two beads on each thread between the rings. To make the earrings, string beads on your thread and then wind the shuttles. Shuttle 2 gets just the smaller beads. These are small pearl beads about the size of seed beads. Fourteen (or 15) small beads for S2.

Shuttle one gets small and larger beads. Three small, one large, 5 Small, one large, five small, one large, and then one small beads go on the thread for S1.

Wind about a yard of thread onto S2, and then pull a yard or two off the ball for S1, CTM.

Wind thread onto the shuttles, CTM, moving the appropriate number of beads to each of the two shuttles. Leave some thread between the two shuttles to work comfortably.

To tat the earrings, follow the Daisy Chain instructions, substituting the small beads for the picots. The first (bottom) ring may have six beads around, or seven as in the Picots of the Earring instructions. Load 15 bead on S2 if doing seven beads on the bottom ring.

The bracelet begins with a small ring to add a clasp when it is finished.

Ring (9) then slide one bead from each shuttle into place before tatting the first ring with the beads. This uses only six of the small beads in the first beaded ring. Seven beads will make it the same size as the other two rings. This is just personal preference.

I tatted 14 of the beaded rings for my bracelet which is about 6" long. I added about 1.5" of chain so that it will easily fit 6.5" to 8" wrists. So, Doing the math to calculate the number of beads required is easy.

S2: 5 beads for each ring. 5 x 14 = 70

S1: 4 sm, 1 lg for the first ring. 5 sm, 1 lg for the remainder of them.

4 Sm 1 lg 5 Sm 1 Lg 5 Sm 1 Lg, etc.

I used 14 Large beads, and 69 Small beads for S1.

This would also make a beautiful necklace or a lanyard. Figure out the length you need, and then how many rings per inch with the beads you choose. Then string the number of beads required for the length you want to make it.

If your shuttle will not easily hold the number of beads you need, you may wish to use a larger shuttle, or load just half of the beads, and then unwind the shuttles when you run out of beads. String the rest of the beads, and rewind the shuttles to continue. This is easier with the bobbin shuttles.

To tat the charm for the end of the chain, string 4 Sm beads for S2, and then 3 Sm 1 Lg 1 Sm for S1. This only requires about a yard of thread, so a bit of leftover thread end works well.

TATTED CHARM

Split Ring (2 B 2 B 2 B 2 /

Lay the S1 thread along the core thread, and then tat over both
threads. B 2 B 2 B 2 B 2)

In the photo on the right, the
first stitch of the second half
of the split ring is completed

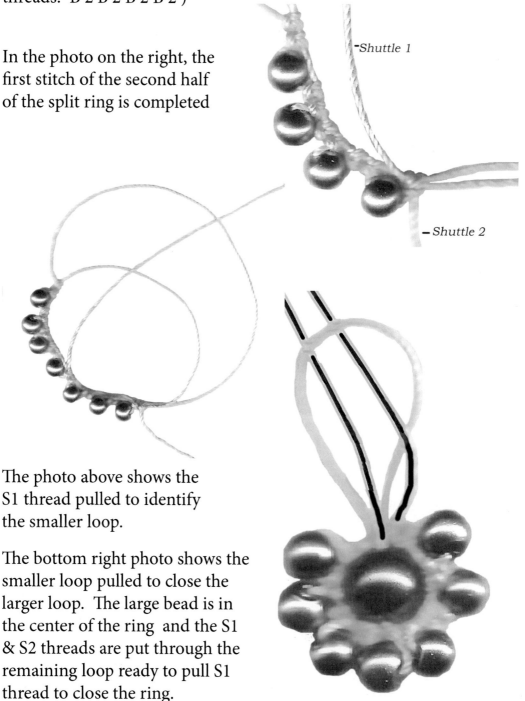

The photo above shows the
S1 thread pulled to identify
the smaller loop.

The bottom right photo shows the
smaller loop pulled to close the
larger loop. The large bead is in
the center of the ring and the S1
& S2 threads are put through the
remaining loop ready to pull S1
thread to close the ring.

41

To add the final bead, string one Sm bead on one thread end, and then put the other thread end through it, but from the opposite direction.

Put one thread end through the last link on a 1.5" piece of chain, and then tat the Split Ring around the link of chain.

Split Ring (4 / put the S1 thread trough the link of chain so that both threads go through the chain. Lay the S1 thread along the core thread, and tat over both threads. 4)

To close this ring, pull the S1 thread to make one of the core loops smaller, and then pull this smaller loop to close the larger loop.

Put the S2 thread through the loop, and pull S1 thread to close the ring completely.

Hide the S2 end, and then cut close to the work. The S1 end is already hidden in the stitches of the second half of the ring.

This photo shows the Split Ring tatted around the last link of the metal chain. Since this is larger I used a paper clip to show the chain.

The smaller loop has been pulled to close the larger loop, so there is only one core loop remaining. The S2 thread is through the loop, and it is ready to pull the S1 thread to completely close the ring.

Notice that the S1 thread end is already hidden in the stitches of the second half of the split ring and can be cut off after the ring is completely closed. Hide the S2 thread end, and then cut it off.

PIRATES BOOTY EARRING

I designed this pattern for the Sunshine State Tat Days 2016. The theme was Gasparilla (Pirates).

The dragonfly beads on the sample shown here is a set of beads purchased from a craft store. This can be tatted with just about any bead combination for the drop bead assembly. Also shown here is a green semi-precious stone, and two coral stone beads.

The tatting is two Split rings or two rings. The finished piece is the same, but the instructions are different, and the beads have to be strung differently to achieve the same end result.

There is more than one way to do most anything.

TWO SPLIT RING OPTION

Begin by deciding on what beads or stones you want to use. This is the fun part! There are lots of colors and possibilities. The 21 small beads are size 11 seed beads, or you may use small pearls, or gemstones. This sample has one semi-precious stone, but you could use anything you wish to make the dangle.

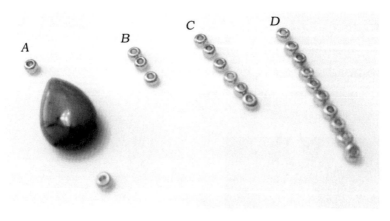

(A) Put a floss threader or bead needle on your thread. Put one seed bead, the drop bead or beads of your choice, and then another seed bead on the thread. Skip the last seed bead and go back through the remaining beads. Slide this assembly to about the middle of the thread.

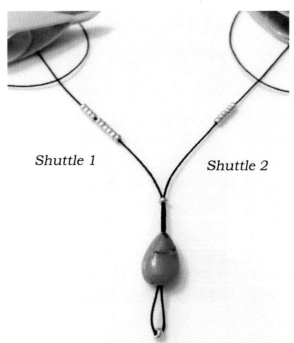

Shuttle 1   Shuttle 2

(B) Set three seed beads aside to use later.

(C) Load six seed beads on Shuttle 2 thread

(D) Load ten seed beads on Shuttle 1 thread

44

Slide one Shuttle 1 seed bead down next to the drop bead assembly before beginning the split ring.

Eight of the Shuttle 1 beads go in the hand ring. One seed bead goes on Shuttle 1.

Split Ring (2 B 2 BBB [This is three beads on a picot. Also slide the one bead from the shuttle thread to make three "up beads" and one "down bead"]

2 B 2/

Slide one seed bead down next to the drop bead assembly from Shuttle 2, and one bead from the hand ring, then continue with the second half of the split ring.

2 B 2 BBB Slide one bead from the hand ring into place to make three "up beads" and one "down bead"
2 B 2)

Close the ring with the final seed bead of the hand ring in place at the top. As shown here.

Put two seed beads of the three that were set aside earlier, onto one thread end, and one seed bead on the other thread end. Put the second thread end through the second bead on the first thread end, but from the opposite direction, as shown below.

Tat a split ring (3 / 3)

Before doing the second half of the split ring lay the Shuttle one thread next to the core thread of the second half and tat the second half over both threads. One thread end is hidden, only one thread end left to hide when finished.

Pull the S1 thread a little to identify the smaller, outer loop, of core thread, then pull this smaller loop thread to close the inner loop, then pull the S1 thread all the way to close the ring.

TWO RING OPTION

Set three seed beads aside to use later. Using a beading needle or a floss threader to load beads onto the shuttle thread:

Six seed beads, Dangle assembly: One seed bead, small bead, large bead, one seed bead Skip the last seed bead and go back through the large bead, small bead, and then the one seed bead, Seven seed beads.

The previous beads are all in the hand ring.
[the thread that goes around the hand to make the ring]

Three more seed beads (these go on the shuttle) See photo below.

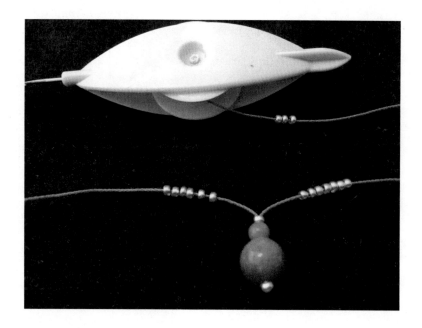

Begin Tatting the Ring

Ring (2 B 2 BBB [slide one bead from the shuttle to make three "up beads" and one "down bead".

2 B 2

B Dangle assembly B [slide one bead from the shuttle to make three "up beads" and one "down bead".

2 B 2 BBB [slide one bead from the shuttle to make three "up beads" and one "down bead".

2 B 2) Close the ring.

One seed bead remains in the hand ring as shown below left.

Add two beads to one thread end, and one to the other thread end, then put the second thread end through the second bead on the first thread end, but from the other direction as in the split ring option.

Tat a ring of 6 DS around an earring finding. THC

The disadvantage to the two ring method of tatting this piece is that the dangle assembly has to slide along the thread until needed

The two split ring option starts with the dangle assembly, so it is in place at the beginning. If tatting something complicated, like the dragonfly beads, it can be fussy to get all those beads to slide around. One thing that will make it easier, would be to put a paperclip on the thread next to the seed bead at the bottom of the dangle beads.

48

CELTIC KNOT RED HAT

One shuttle and ball CTM with red thread in any size.

Begin with a picot by tying an over hand knot in the thread between the shuttle and ball. Tat the first stitch of a chain a picot's distance from the knot.
Chain – 18 – 18 – 18 – 18

These chain sections are tatted fairly tight so that they loop over and under as shown in the diagram at the right.   Join to the beginning picot, and then continue tatting.
Chain 2 – 2 – 2 – 2 – 2 +
(Repeat around 3 more times)

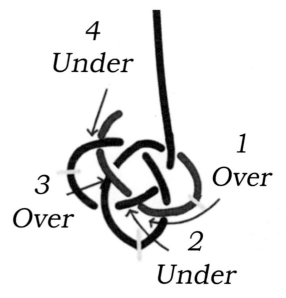

This will make the top part of the hat form a cup shape and the Celtic knot look like a woven straw hat.

Ring 3 – 2 + 2 – 3
Join to a picot of the previous round.

Repeat around and join the last ring to the split ring picot at the beginning of the brim. THC

Add one ring flowers and feather, then attach an earring finding to one of the chains of the brim.

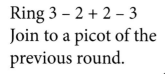

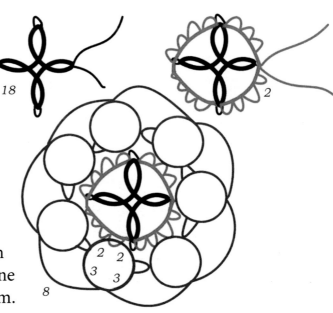

CELTIC FUNKY CHICKEN

Just gotta LOVE chickens!

I taught an Easy Celtic Knot class at Fringe Element Tat Days 2012, and this chicken hatched out of the instructions... sort of.

Use any color thread, even variegated thread if you wish to tat an exotic bird.

There are 15 seed beads in the trefoil knot, five for each wing, and five for the tail. The feet have three beads each, and there are three seed beads for the beak. I used size 20 thread to make an earring.

Trefoil knot:
String 15 beads on the ball thread, and then wind a yard or so onto a shuttle, CTM.

Slide three beads between the ball and shuttle and then tat one DS on the other side of these beads, which will put the beads in a picot at the beginning of the chain as shown in the photo below.

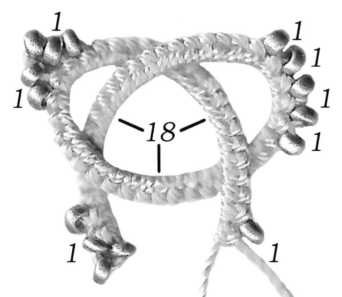

Chain BBB 1 B 18

B 1 BBB 1 B 18

B 1 B 1 B 1 B 1 B

18 B 1
Weave the trefoil knot as shown, and then tie the thread ends at the beginning of the chain. Hide the ends, cut.

The photo on the right shows the trefoil knot completed.

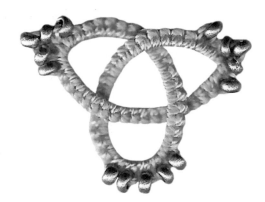

To tat the body, head, and legs use two shuttles CTM. String the nine beads on the thread, and then wind the shuttles.

S 1 Body chain - 18
Leave a thread space the size of five DS and tat the foot.
Put three beads in the hand ring.
S 2 Ring (2 B 2 B 2 B 2)
Put a loop of thread or a paper clip through the foot to make it easy to hold on to while tatting the Chain 5 unflipped DS on the thread space for the leg.

S 1 Chain 2 then tat another leg and foot like before.

Chain 15 and then weave this through the trefoil knot as shown below. Join to the beginning picot.

Neck: Chain 3 Turn

Head: Three beads in the hand ring.

Ring (12
[Daisy Picot with red 1 - 1 - 1 - 1]
4 B B B 3)

Make a Larks Head knot at the bottom of the beak, and cut it so it is about the same as in the photo at the right.

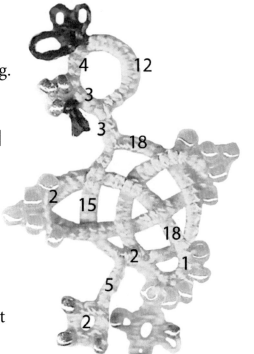

Hide the thread ends and then cut close to the work.
Add an earring finding.

51

CELTIC KNOT MOON

This Celtic knot moon is a challenge. The sample is size 8 Pearle cotton, and is about 1.5" tall. There are clusters of three seed beads at the top and bottom.

String 6 seed beads on the ball thread, and then wind a yard or so of thread on a shuttle, CTM.

Begin a chain with a picot by tying a knot between the ball and shuttle, and then tat the first stitch a picot's distance from the knot. The picot is the beginning of the chain directions below.

Chain - 15 - 30 - 15 - 16 - 16 - 15 - 30 - 15 - 16

Weave the bottom knot shown in the photo below first, and then the other knot shown woven in this photo. Do the weaving so that your piece looks exactly like the photo below. Next, continue tatting.

Chain + 16
This is the progress shown in the photo at the right. You can not do the join and the rest of the tatting until weaving those Celtic knots!

Now weave the other two Celtic knots so that the piece looks like the photos. These are all just the Celtic trefoil knots. You should be able to easily follow the "over, under, over, under" weaving pattern.
Join to the beginning picot.

Just do the first half of a lock join. Next, tie a SLT in the two threads to change the position of the shuttle and ball thread so that they are in the right place to continue tatting around the outside of the knots.

Chain 3 BBB 8

Tighten the tension so that the three beads make a nice point at the top of the moon.

You may either finger tat, or put the thread on a needle (a tapestry needle works) and then use the needle as if it were a shuttle.

The rest of the joins on this piece are just putting the core thread through the picots, and
continuing with the stitches. This will make the outline smooth.

Chain + 8 + 8 + 8 + 8 + 8 + 8 + 8

BBB 3

Tie the ends in the picot at the point of the final Celtic knot. Hide the ends and cut close to the work.

Add an earring finding with a jump ring.

CELTIC STAR

This Celtic five point Star is tatted in one round. The sample here is size 8 Pearle cotton. It is 1.25" across.

String 12 seed beads on the ball thread, and then wind a yard or two of thread on a Celtic shuttle, CTM.

Begin a chain with a picot by tying a knot between the ball and shuttle. Tat the first stitch a picot's distance from the knot.

Chain - 13 turn

Ring A (2 - 2 - 2) turn

Chain 13 BBB 13 turn

Ring B (2 - 2 - 2) turn

Chain 13 BBB 13 turn

Ring C (2 - 2 + 2) turn
This join is to the picot of Ring A
See photo at the right.

Chain 13 BBB 13 turn

Ring D (2 + 2 + 2) turn

Chain 13 BBB 13 turn

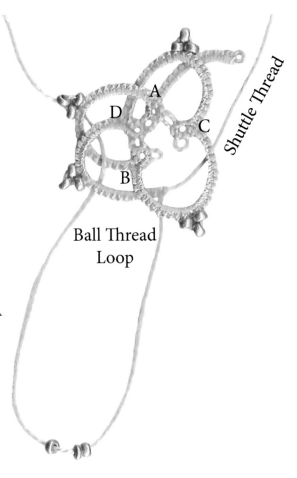

The photo on the bottom of the previous page shows the progress this far with the shuttle woven through the chains between Rings A & B.

Pull the ball thread through the previous work as shown.

The photo diagram at the right shows how the thread and tatting are woven through.

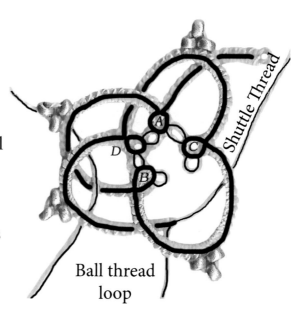

The ball thread loop is not all shown, but is the same as in the previous photo.

Fold the chain between rings B & C up, out of the way, to make it easier to tat Ring E.

Ring E (2 + 2 + 2) Turn
The joins are to the picots of Ring B & Ring C.

Chain 13

Cut the thread ends to about 12 inches, and then weave the last chain through the chain between Rings B & C. Pull the ball thread end through the tatting.

Tie the ends through the beginning picot. String two seed beads on one thread end, and one on the other. Pull the thread end with one bead on it through the second bead of the other thread, but from the opposite direction to make the cluster of three beads at the top of the star.

Tat a small ring around an earring finding as in the other patterns in this book. Hide the ends and then cut them off close to the work.

CELTIC THREE RING WREATH

This wreath is tatted as three separate interlocked rings. It could be done in three colors, or three of the same color or even variegated colors.

I have used clusters of three gold colored beads, but single red beads would look like a traditional Christmas wreath.

Begin the first ring by stringing six beads on the thread of one shuttle. Wind about a yard or two on the shuttle. The six beads go in the hand ring.

BDS Ring A (9 BBB 18 BBB 9)
Close the ring and hide the ends, then cut close to the work.

Put the thread for the next ring through Ring A two times, as shown below. When the tatting is finished, pull the tatting through the ring to arrange the tatting around the previous ring where the thread goes.

Second Ring: String six beads on the thread.
BDS Ring B (9 BBB 18 BBB 9)
Arrange the tatting so that it is woven through the first ring, and then
close the ring and hide the ends. Cut close to the work.

Third Ring: Put the thread for the next ring through the two previous
rings two times as shown above. I used black thread so it would be
easier to see.

String three beads on the thread.
BDS Ring C (18 BBB 18)

Close the ring, and arrange the
three rings so that the bead clusters
are evenly spaced around.

Put two beads on one thread end,
and one bead on the other. Put
the thread end with one bead
through the second bead on the
other thread, but from the opposite
direction as shown on the right.

Slide the beads down next to the
tatting, and tat a split ring around
an earring finding.

Terms & Notation

-	Picot
+	Join to a previously tatted picot.
B	Bead, BBB means three beads together.
B+	Add a bead when making a join.
BDS Ring	A tatted ring of all Balanced Double Stitches.
BDS	Balanced double stitch. A DS with an extra turn around the core thread for each half of the stitch.
Chain ##	Tat a chain of ## DS where ## indicates how many DS.
CTM	Continuous Thread Method – do not cut the thread between the ball and shuttle or between two shuttles.
D	First half of Double Stitch
Dora Young Knot	Also called Split chain, or Bridging: a method of making a DS or larks head knot without having to put the shuttle through a space that is too small for the shuttle.
DS	Tatting stitch or double stitch.
Hand Ring	The thread that goes around your hand when tatting a ring.
Josephine Ring	A tatted ring made with a complete double stitch at the beginning and the end but just the first half of DS in between them.
Ring (2 – 2)	Tat a ring of. 2 DS, a picot, 2 DS, and then close the ring.
S	Second half of Double Stitch.
SLT	Shoe Lace Trick: tie a knot in the two threads.
Split Ring	A ring that starts at one place and ends at another place.
THC	Tie the thread ends. Hide the ends. Cut them off.
Turn	Reverse work or flip it over